KAPUAPUA'S MAGIC SHELL

by Joe Adair
illustrated by Paula Zinngrabe Wendland

PEARSON

Scott Foresman

Editorial Offices: Glenview, Illinois • Parsippany, New Jersey • New York, New York
Sales Offices: Needham, Massachusetts • Duluth, Georgia • Glenview, Illinois
Coppell, Texas • Ontario, California • Mesa, Arizona

Far out in the Pacific Ocean a man sailed his small canoe. The sail caught the wind, and the waves pushed it towards a small island. The island looked tiny because it was so far away.

The man in the canoe was Kapuapua. Kapuapua was an old Hawaiian man who had spent many years sailing from island to island in the Pacific Ocean. He was looking for food and good drinking water. He was hungry and thirsty. The wind hit his sail, and the waves carried him closer to shore.

Kapuapua was a kind and gentle old man. He had long white hair, thick bushy eyebrows, and a big belly. Kapuapua knew many stories. Children loved to sit around him and listen to his stories.

Kapuapua's canoe was getting very close to the shore. He smelled the wonderful aroma coming from the beautiful flowers on the island. He decided that this was an island he wanted to visit.

Kapuapua's canoe slid onto the sandy beach. He laughed to himself. He loved being on land again.

Some of the children from the island saw him. They ran to tell their parents about the strange old man. Many of the parents were upset because someone had landed on their island. They believed that this stranger would ask them for food and water. Because he was not one of them, they did not want to share their food or water with him.

Kapuapua smelled cooking food. He followed his nose and ended up at the edge of the village. People saw him and they hid their food.

Kapuapua walked to the first house. A woman named Howina asked him what he wanted. Kapuapua very politely asked for some food and water.

Howina pointed to the stream and said, "You can find water over there, but there is no food in this village." Kapuapua walked over to the stream and drank a lot of water. Now he really needed food.

After drinking water, Kapuapua went to the next house. There, he asked for some food. A man named Iz told him to go away. The same thing happened at every house in the village. The people did not want to share food with a stranger.

Soon it became dark and started to rain. No one let this poor old man stay in their home. So Kapuapua fell asleep under a coconut tree.

The next morning Kapuapua felt
something hit his head. It was a coconut
that fell from the tree. It hurt a little, but it
gave him a wonderful idea!

Kapuapua had a plan to get food from
the villagers. He needed his magic seashell
though. So he walked back to the beach
and took the seashell out of his canoe.

Kapuapua walked to the center of the
village and began to make a fire under a
large black cooking pot.

Kapuapua lit a fire and poured water
from the stream into the big pot. Howina
asked him what he was doing. He told her
he was making his magic seashell soup.

"Magic seashell soup. Whatever in the
world is that?" Howina asked.

He laughed. Soon the children joined
her. Kapuapua explained that many years
ago he met a famous king and went to a
great feast with him. Kapuapua cooked his
magic seashell soup for the king. The king
loved it!

Kapuapua continued with the story. He told the villagers, "As soon as the water boils, I will make a pot of magic soup." But, he told them, they could not have any of his soup. There was only enough for one person.

Soon the villagers asked if they could add some food of their own. Then there would be enough for them to taste. Kapuapua just smiled and kept on stirring.

Kapuapua picked up the seashell. He was the only one who knew it was just a regular shell that he found a long time ago. He dropped it into the water. A little splash jumped from the pot and landed on the back of his hand. The people watched as he licked his hand. Then he said, "Mmm, this soup is going to be great!"

Soon the villagers begged for a taste. Kapuapua told them they could have a taste if they added other ingredients to the pot. They asked what they could add to the mixture. Kapuapua asked Iz to bring some fish and Howina to get some nice green vegetables for the soup.

Soon the whole village was lined up with all sorts of delicious seafoods, green vegetables, and sweet fruits. Kapuapua added them to the pot.

He told them about the man at the king's party who roasted a whole pig for the party. Just then a man from the village said, "I have a pig. If I roast it for the villagers, will you let me taste the magic seashell soup?" Kapuapua said yes and continued with his story. He told them about men and women who sang beautiful songs and played lovely music.

Some young people asked Kapuapua if they could taste his soup if they danced and played music. Again, his big, round stomach jiggled as he laughed loudly and said yes!

Kapuapua then asked the villagers if they had a bakery. They didn't know what he meant. So he told the villagers about a good sweet bread they should make for dessert. Some of the villagers asked how to make it. Kapuapua told them how to make the dough for the bread.

　　Kapuapua asked some young men
to take over stirring the batch of soup.
The pot was getting so full that it was
difficult to stir. Other young people of
the village began to play wonderful music
and dance. Kapuapua could smell the
seashell soup and roasting pig in the air.
He smiled and watched as other villagers
cut up pineapples and other fruit. Then
he walked over to the men and women
making the dough for the sweet bread.
He showed them how to knead it. Then
he told them to make it into long logs and
braid it together.

After the dough was kneaded and braided, the villagers put it in the village oven to bake. Kapuapua told them to take it out when the bread was golden brown. And he told them to sprinkle sugar on top. It was going to be a very delicious dessert.

The villagers put a table near the soup pot. Next to it they placed the breads, fruit, and the roasted pig. Kapuapua walked over to the huge black pot and tasted some of the soup. He smiled and told everyone that the soup was ready. Then he went and sat back down. But Iz and Howina asked him to be the first to have some of the soup, roasted pig, and fresh fruit. Their feelings for Kapuapua had completely changed. They happily pulled him forward and handed him food. He laughed and filled his big jiggling belly!

There was so much food, laughter, dancing, and music. It was wonderful to be at the village for this feast. The weather was just right and everyone sat outside. They ate and talked. Some of the villagers got up and danced. And others gathered around Kapuapua asking him to tell more stories about the places he had visited.

Everyone was having a wonderful time. They ate the whole roasted pig, all the delicious vegetables, and fresh fruit. The children were playing games as their parents watched and smiled. The young men and women danced all night long to the wonderful music. After the food was eaten, Kapuapua called for the sweet bread to be brought out for dessert. The children were first in line because they loved sweet treats like this.

Kapuapua rested under a palm tree. The wise and loving smile on his face made him look like a benevolent king. The villagers treated him like one, too. They brought him more food and asked him to tell more stories. Kapuapua told them about his exciting adventures on other islands. This gentle and kindly old man with long white hair and a big belly laughed with great joy because he felt just like a king.

A Hawaiian Luau

Kapuapua was a very kind and loving Hawaiian man. He loved to laugh and share his stories with other people. He also loved to eat other people's food!

The feast that we read about in this story is a **luau**. A luau is a Hawaiian term that describes a party with a lot of good food. The roasted pig is cooked underground in a special oven called an *imu.*

Because Hawaii is made up of many islands, there are many kinds of seafood at a luau. Most luaus also have delicious Hawaiian sweet bread. Kapuapua showed the villagers how to make such a dessert.

Luaus also have Hawaiian music and dancing. The story you read gives you a good idea of how much fun a real luau can be!